D0213981

THAT SWING

Johns Hopkins: Poetry and Fiction

John T. Irwin, General Editor

Also by X. J. Kennedy

The Bestiary, by Guillaume Apollinaire (translation)
In a Prominent Bar in Secaucus: New and Selected Poems,
 1955–2007
The Lords of Misrule
Dark Horses

Swing

Poems, 2008–2016

X. J. Kennedy

JOHNS HOPKINS UNIVERSITY PRESS | BALTIMORE

This book has been brought to publication with the generous assistance of the Poetry and Fiction Fund.

© 2017 X. J. Kennedy
All rights reserved. Published 2017
Printed in the United States of America on acid-free paper
9 8 7 6 5 4 3 2 1

Johns Hopkins University Press
2715 North Charles Street
Baltimore, Maryland 21218-4363
www.press.jhu.edu

Library of Congress Cataloging-in-Publication Data

Names: Kennedy, X. J., author.
Title: That swing : poems, 2008–2016 / X. J. Kennedy.
Description: Baltimore : Johns Hopkins University Press, [2017] |
    Series: Johns Hopkins: Poetry and Fiction
Identifiers: LCCN 2016035399| ISBN 9781421422442 (pbk. : alk. paper) |
    ISBN 1421422441 (pbk. : alk. paper) | ISBN 9781421422459 (electronic)
    | ISBN 142142245X (electronic)
Classification: LCC PS3521.E563 A6 2017 | DDC 811/.54—dc23
    LC record available at https://lccn.loc.gov/2016035399

A catalog record for this book is available from the British Library.

*Special discounts are available for bulk purchases of this book. For more
information, please contact Special Sales at 410-516-6936 or specialsales
@press.jhu.edu.*

Johns Hopkins University Press uses environmentally friendly book
materials, including recycled text paper that is composed of at least 30
percent post-consumer waste, whenever possible.

for Dorothy
as always

It Don't Mean a Thing (If It Ain't Got That Swing)

—*Duke Ellington*

CONTENTS

I   Recollections

Lonesome George

Giant tortoise kept penned at the Darwin Research Station,
Puerto Ayora, Galápagos Islands

No mate for him exists.
    Last one of his subspecies,
he solemnly persists
    in turning into feces
eelgrass brown and dry,
    spine-sprinkled cactus leaves.
Straining to gulp a fly
    dejectedly retrieves
blunt head. Dead-ending male,
    lone emblem of despair,
he slumps on his kneecaps, tail
    antennaing the air.
For a long moment we bind
    sympathetic looks,
we holdouts of our kind,
    like rhymed lines, printed books.

My Mother Consigns to the Flames My Trove of Comic Books

for Helen Webber

BLAM went the planet Krypton. One child fled
By spaceship, grew up to be Superman
Whose X-ray eyes could ogle Lois Lane
Right through her dress. My mother grimly fed
The furnace with my funnybooks—"Such trash
To waste your money on!" I saw flames scorch
Batman and Robin, watched the Human Torch
Sizzle and twist like bacon, and the Flash
In a flash leap to ashes. Oh, chagrin.

Had she preserved in bank vaults, not cremated
Those hidden treasures, might they have been fated
To fetch a fortune? Ah, it might have been,
Or not have been. How can we know which art
The whimsical future will decide to cherish?
Those superguys I loved were bound to perish.
I would have read them till they fell apart.

The Odors of New Jersey

Not those of glum Perth Amboy's massive clump
Of oil refineries, tar fumes, sulfur heaps
Inspiring travelers Philadelphia-bound
To clamp their nostrils, tromp hard on the gas,
Nor nowadays whatever fragrance leaks
From doubtless spotless labs that line the Pike
Where alchemists in white coats synthesize
Aromas of fast food
To make you swear there's beef fat in your fries.

No, let me keep instead
Peaches revolving backsides to the sun,
Mooning their frizzy cheeks, a Sunday feast
Of pullets from Ironia stuffed with sage,
The knock-you-over whiff of fishing boats
Docking with holds athrash in Manasquan,
Tear-jerking onions chopped for chili sauce,
The pungent come-on of dime store perfume
From Gloria's earlobe in a darkened room
That night we kids played spin-the-bottle games,
She standing on toe tips,
My dumb hands clumsily rummaging,
Prospecting wildly for each other's lips.

Hopes

While we'd sit, eager for a movie show,
Chaplin or Betty Boop on the home projector,
My mother used to swear—a slapping sound
When the film snapped, its loose end spinning round;
And when at last my scheme delivered Muriel
Tipsy, spread-eagled in my double bed,
Damn. I'd forgot the condom. And she gurgled,
"Pull out, you fool! I teach Planned Parenthood!"

The tendency of high hopes to abort
Is our condition: in the cancer center
That abrupt moment when you're drawn up short,
Having expected life to keep going on,
Like starting to take the last sip from your wineglass
Only to find the wine already gone.

Insanity in the Basement

The smell of fish guts finned our basement air
Where my old man in his sprung-springed easy chair
Used to consume his Sunday morning feast,
Bloaters he'd toast
On a shovel over furnace coals, not daring
To bring upstairs that evil-smelling herring.
And when fish-hating Uncle Norman's reel
Cranked in a tuna fit for Gargantua's meal,
Who had to be that fish's glad receiver?
My old man. Whipped out his butcher's cleaver
And in our basement took a vicious whack
At its backbone, causing the blade
To take off into space. It made
Straight for my mother, missed her by an inch.
She wasn't one to flinch
But drily said, *Good shot.*

And then that lot
Of cage-kept rabbits, their endearing capers
Vulnerable to coal gas vapors,
So that the neighbors swore they set their clocks
By Mother's trips each dawn with spade and box
Out to our garden graveyard. Once, my Uncle Bill

Flipped and became a gabbling, twitchy shell
Until his poor wife could no longer stand him,
Said to my mother, *Here, you understand him,*
And lent him for the summer. In our basement
He'd sleep on the mohair sofa by the casement
That let in rain. Said the perfume of coal
Calmed him. Indeed, by Labor Day his soul
Grew whole again. At last he ceased to quiver.
In dreams I still hear Johnson's Coal deliver
Our coming winter's heat in a deafening rain:
Down a short steel chute, a two-ton hurricane.

Literacy

remembering Caroline Bray Kennedy

Her lips worked hard, pronouncing every word
Without a sound. Forefinger slowly traced
Each line, and at the end of Revelations,
She'd pause a moment, turn back to creation's
First lightburst, and set out to read again.

Her Cornish speech took cadence from the style
Of King James verse, and held on to it late,
Her chosen words a softly trickling brook.
Though nowadays my bookshelves creak with weight,
Compared to her, I haven't read a book.

Progress

Sundays we'd stroll to the railroad track,
My white-collared father and I,
Where he'd gaze after freight trains billowing past
And deliver him of a sigh—

"If I still worked for the railroad
I'd retire with a pass. I could ride
To any place in the country
And the country, they say, is wide."

Yet for thirty years my father
With fountain pen wielded power
At the boiler factory in Dover
Keeping track of each man-hour:

He would total up columns of numbers
In a flash with astonishing skill
And never a man's pay envelope
Fell short of a dollar bill.

He would hike to the bank every Thursday
To fetch payroll cash in a sack,

The insurance company insisting
That a blue steel pistol he pack.

How the neighbors would taunt and tease him—
"Hey, Joe, would you pull your gun
And shoot it out with a stickup man?"—
"I'd throw him the money and run."

He continued to add up numbers
In his head till there came on the scene
A formidable robot rival,
The Burroughs adding machine.

Then my father saw that his number
Would shortly be up. As he feared,
Anybody could tug on a handle
And an accurate total appeared.

They broke the news to him gently,
They professed their profound regret
And presented him, not with a pension,
With a pen and pencil set.

For a time he displayed it proudly
Till the pencil had to be tossed
When it wouldn't quite twist as it used to
And the cap of the pen got lost.

11

For more than eight thousand mornings
He had walked to his job past a sign
Where the Women's Christian Temperance
Union had posted a line

Ill fitting the situation
Of the obsolescently skilled:
Life is no goblet to be drained
But a measure to be filled.

Early Morning in Turks and Caicos Hospital

A bleating wail crawls down the corridor,
A native infant tugged forth from the womb,
Unsure that daylight was worth waiting for.
Ahead lies heartbreak interspersed with joy,
Unfulfilled hopes, toil, grinding poverty,
A life spent at the mercy of the sea.
Here's better luck than likely to you, boy.
If I could drink, I'd toast your health in wine,
But your own dad will drink to his new son.
You gasp for breath, your footrace just begun,
Unlike us who draw near the finish line.
My right hand wanders down as if to feel
My cold new hip joint of titanium steel.

2 Saints and Others

Three Saints

After miniatures from Henry VIII's Book of Hours

for Stephen Sandy

1. MARTHA

"Oh, come along, you silly beast," she clucked.
"Now don't you gobble people anymore."
Obedient, the Tarasque, looking whacked,
Waddled behind her trying to ignore
The yeoman with rock-steady crossbow drawn
Upon the monster's right eye and the knight
Driving his lance into its scaly brawn
As if brute nature might submit to might.

Two limp legs dangled from its lower jaw,
For it was nothing if not fully fed,
And yet the haloed saint had thrown a rope
About its neck. Triumphantly, she led
It like a poodle: "Come, obey God's law,
And like our own dear king, ignore the Pope."

2. CATHERINE

Condemned to perish on a wooden wheel,
She hears her bones snap as she's stretched out lean,
But God thinks twice, sends down a miracle—
A vicious flash. And no more vile machine,

No more tormenters. Catherine's appeal
Soared far beyond her purity of heart:
Her name rose, fastened to a firework wheel
That whistled round and round and flew apart.

You'd think that would have earned her permanence
Among the blest, but her devotion ceases
When Paul the Sixth finds little evidence
That she has been, and lets her fly to pieces.

3. NICHOLAS

Just born, still swaddled in umbilical cord,
Nicholas leaped to his feet, cried "Praise the Lord!"—
A fast start. Once when a hard-up neighbor
Couldn't raise dowries, only sinful labor
Loomed for his daughters till the good saint tossed
Into their bed a ball of purest gold,
Preventing them from being bought and sold.

And when a vile innkeeper, soused on wine,
Figuring human victims to be cheaper
Than beef to feed his guests, butchered three boys
And soaked their bodies in a vat of brine,
It took the godly Nicholas to revive
Them with a blessing, bring 'em back alive
With salt tastes in their mouths, but no regrets—
A miracle to be remembered. Let's
Seek refuge in the bosom of Saint Nicholas
Should anybody ever try to pickle us.

Jane Austen Drives to Alton
in Her Donkey Trap

Disappointing waters at Cheltenham Spa
Hadn't erased dark patches from her skin,
Nor could she still walk miles untiringly.
Out back she harnessed Polly Sue
And set off briskly through a warmth that May
Would squander on dregs of day.

"Composition seems to me impossible," she said,
"With a head full of doses of rhubarb
And joints of mutton"—
Nevertheless, on that rough road back to Chawton,
She closed a stubborn sentence in her mind
As one might fasten a button.

Looming, the near-horizon wore a hue
Softer than garnet's, fullness she might carry,
The first shy sycamore leaves
Uncertainly poking through
Like the affections of a girl
Whose mother hadn't decreed which man to marry.

With faithful clop her donkey drew a load
Of oolong, sugar, pink embroidery thread,
Her quiet drive portending one last story.
Today, our rented compact squeezes left,
Scrapes weeds and fence posts while around the road's
Blind bend down thunderstorms a ten-ton lorry.

Thomas Hardy's Obsequies

When Hardy perished, torn between
A Dorset graveyard and the Abbey,
Folks whispered a peculiar tale
Whose central figure was a tabby.

It was decreed that Hardy burn
And satisfy each bookish mourner
By being honored with an urn
Of ashes in the Poets' Corner,

But he had chosen other ground,
His native earth, in which to rest,
And so a compromise was found:
A surgeon probed the great man's breast,

Dispatched inside a biscuit tin
His excised heart out to the yard
Of Stinsford Church for placement in
Ground that his forebears' gravestones guard.

But soon the sexton coming for
The poet's disembodied pumper

Found the tin empty on the floor,
The house cat grinning, belly plumper.

Well, what to do? Despairing not,
They sheared the cat of all nine lives,
Interred her in a flowered plot
Flanked by the first and second wives,
.

A fate that Hardy might have planned,
Ironic—he'd have relished that—
A wife on either handless hand,
A heart whose casket is a cat.

A Word from Hart Crane's Ghost

Why did I leap?
You may well wonder. Sleep
With a woman and you build a bridge
Across two minds, two bodies, inch by inch—

God, I was tired.
The whole steel cognizance swung round and backfired.
The sucking Gulf seemed, oh,
A deep green cinch.

In Tiananmen Square

In a mausoleum Chairman Mao
Outlasting late attacks
Still lies embalmed. Nowadays he looks
Fashioned of orange wax.

Floral displays he would have banned
Brighten the square's right border.
Policemen verify IDs
Which had best be in order.

Tourists strike poses, shutters click,
Arrest the fountain's spray.
The pavement gleams, intently scrubbed,
Blood long since sponged away.

Mao's countenance still held on high
Looks down where once had lain
Young dissidents whose lightless eyes
Protested being slain.

3 Versions

Sonnet for Hélène

after Pierre de Ronsard

When thou art old, with night fast drawing nigh,
   Spinning, thy chair beside the crackling flame,
    Utter my lines, remember that acclaim
Ronsard once gave thy beauty long gone by.
Then shalt thou have no servant blind or lame,
   Sunken in sleep or nodding at his chores,
   Who'll not leap to fling open wide the doors,
And go forth shouting praises to thy name.

In earth I'll be buried, a ghost without bone,
   In cypress-deepened shadows I'll abide,
And thou by the hearth, a gray stooped-over crone,
   Will rue my love and thy disdainful pride.
    Dear one, delay no longer. Gather ye
    From this day forth the roses of To Be.

Abyss

after Charles Baudelaire

Wherever Pascal went went his abyss
    Like a good dog. All's chasm now: wish, word,
    Dream, deed. Over my hair that when it's scared
Rears upright on its roots I feel wind cross.
Up, down, around me—fathomlessness, loss,
    Silence, seductive space. On night's blackboard
    The professorial finger of the Lord
Traces unending nightmares, and I toss,
Leery of sleep as of some gaping pit
    Oozing with spooks that leads down who knows where.
My windows open on the infinite;
    Vertigo shrieks inside me, and my soul's
    Jealous of voids: at least, they're unaware,
    Not jailed by all these beings, numerals!

Sea Breeze

after Stéphane Mallarmé

My flesh is glum. I've read up all the books.
Good God, I've got to get out of here. The rooks
Thirst for fresh ocean foam and drunken skies.
No ancient garden mirrored in my eyes
Can hold this heart here that the sea makes damp,
No night, nor the lonesome glimmer of my lamp
On vacant paper, whiteness guarding it,
Nor my young wife who gives our child the tit.
I'm off. Hey, schooner balancing your mast,
Lift anchor for some spicy isle, but fast.
Boredom laid desolate by hopes and griefs
Still longs for the last farewells of handkerchiefs.
Perhaps this frail hull beckons hostile gales
That romp across lost ships and tattered sails,
Vessels from fertile islands torn apart—
But oh, hear the songs the sailors sing you, heart!

Because the Dinner Meat Was Done to Death

after Stéphane Mallarmé

Because the dinner meat was done to death,
    Because the news told of a woman raped,
Because the chambermaid forgot to shut
    Her buttons and her bulging bosom gaped,
Because from bed vast as a sacristy
    He spies the clock's design—two ancient goats—
Because, when he can't sleep, immodestly
    Under the sheets his leg to her leg floats,

A moron mounts his dry stick of a wife,
    Scrapes with his sweating brow her sleeping cap,
And falls to fucking, gasping for dear life.
    Because he fanned the weak flame of his urge
One calm and sleepless night, in nine months' time
    A Dante or a Shakespeare may emerge.

My Bohemia: A Fantasy

after Arthur Rimbaud

I'd set out, fists in tattered pockets crammed,
    My worn coat turning to a mere idea
    Of a coat, under the sky—to you, Muse, loyal,
And oh! the splendid love trysts to be dreamed!
My only pair of pants would show my skin.
    Tom Thumb-sized dreamer, I'd keep strewing rhymes,
The Great Bear constellation for my inn,
    The stars relinquishing their tinkling chimes.

    And seated by the highway side I'd feel,
        On fine September evenings, drops of dew
        Needle my brow like wine alive with fire;
    While, rhyming in the midst of shadows weird,
        I'd pluck the laces of each holey shoe
        Close to my heart, like playing on a lyre.

Pierrot's Soliloquy

after Jules Laforgue

All I am is a clown in the moon
    Plunking pebbles in fountain pools with
No particular hope, no design
    Except one: to make myself myth.

In defiance I roll back from pale
    Mandarin flesh a sleeve white as rice.
From my circular mouth I exhale
    Crucifixlike my dulcet advice.

But oh to be legend at last
    On the charlatan centuries' threshold!
Ah, but where are the moons of the past?
    Even God—isn't He growing old?

Last Poem

after Robert Desnos

I have so fiercely dreamed of you,
Walked on so far and spoken of you so,
Loving a shade of you so hard
That now I've nothing left of you.
I'm left a shade among the shades,
A hundred times more shade than shade,
A shade cast time and time again
Into your sun-transfigured life.

Mortal Landscape

after Robert Sabatier

The bird is flown, the monster not yet born.
Where shall we go in this demolished world?
We lie here in position waiting death,
Flesh to flesh folded in decrepit light,
Weary of walking forth to meet fresh dawns.

Between man and his shadow there remains
A hairbreadth crack through which loose days slip by.
Ferocious stars, suns that sink teeth in worlds—
I plant the stolen dagger of my cry
Into that breast where godhead walks its rounds.

Each fit of grief delivers me to joy.
Murder or peace—which am I waiting for?
Faces lie hidden in the brake of words,
Faces I fear, that any spring will serve
To drive forth into the pasture of my lines.

The bird is flown, no look lifts off the ground.
I seek in earth a hole where in eclipse

I'll sleep. So many bodies dreamless lie
That what in man is man has had to die
And even words at last make meals on lips.

4 Diversions

Riposte

The poetry editor Quinn
Likes poems that are shapely and thin,
*   And not about owls,*
*   Nebraska, your bowels,*
Or personal redemption from sin.

—Garrison Keillor, "A Fan's Notes"

Sleepless and lone, I'm bolted in my cell
In FoodFuel Nebraska's Winking Owl Motel.
On the tarred roof begin insistent rains
Of mouse bones by some snapping beak let fall.
A neighbor's snores and constipated moans
Worm through the plywood wall.

Bald light bulb sizzles. Faint tap at my door,
Whisper: *Hey mister, you the guy that call*
Min's Escorts? Snap back lock, admit a hag
Mole-cheeked, unnatural blonde of sixty-five
Atilt on high heels, toting beaded bag.
Desireé's here. But will desire arrive?

Of what use absolution if no sin
Take place to give it reason? Sequined blouse

Comes briskly off, now—wow!—her bra's undone.
O Lord, how few the teeth beneath her grin.
An owl hoots twice. I watch a scooting louse
Circle the floor. We clink a round of gin.

Dawn jimmies open eyelids. Sunlight caws
Through stiff Nebraska cornstalks—must have dreamed
That midnight tryst. Grope out of bed, dump bowels,
Wash quaking hands, dry off on threadbare towels,
Commune on stale buns, coffee powder-creamed,
And hit the road, from mortal sin redeemed.

Disabled Music

Ever since our clock that sang
A different birdcall for each hour
Slid from its nail and hit the floor
It hasn't been right in the head. The owl
Whimpers at midnight, and at two
The blue jay squeaks. The Baltimore oriole
Sings as though a heavy boot
Were splintering its skull;
The cardinal, like a rabbit put
To rack and screw. We'd throw it out
Except that some diversity
In telling time seems right—
Who'd not respect
A song delivered in adversity?

.

On a Young Man's Remaining
an Undergraduate for Twelve Years

Sweet scent of pot, the mellow smell of beer,
    Frat-house debates on sex, on God's existence
Lasting all night, vacations thrice a year,
    Pliant coeds who put up brief resistance

Are all life was. Who'd give a damn for earning,
    Who'd struggle by degrees to lofty places
When he can loll, adrift in endless learning,
    In a warm sea of academic stasis?

He's famous now: the everlasting kid.
    After conducting an investigation,
Two deans resigned, to do just what he did.
    They couldn't fault his ratiocination.

Cold Beer at the Paul Revere Capture Site

Revere might have been glad to quaff a brew
That day the Hessians dragged him from his horse
On the battle road, so that he never warned
The Concord farmers of that redcoat force

Slogging toward them. It fell to young Sam Prescott
To carry on the ride with far less fame
Than drop-out Paul has had. Who knows his name,
Fast-horsed alarmist in a fancy waistcoat?

Just come from courting lovely Lydia Mulliken,
He chanced to meet Revere. Unlucky Paul
Had to return on foot to Lexington,
But Prescott spurred his mount, leaped a stone wall

And spread that fateful warning far and near.
Longfellow didn't write, of course, "A tisket,
A tasket—listen up, kids, and you'll hear
Of the midnight ride of Doctor Samuel Prescott."

Sweating in mid-July, we lug a basket
Of cold cans to this site to toast Revere,

The loser, and brave messenger Sam Prescott,

Who unknown to the world deserves a beer.

5   Easters

Invitation to the Dance

First birdsongs in Peaceful Grove. Mabel O'Lannihan
Pitches her blanket, commences to waltz.
Mag O'Quinn with her cane beats time on a bedpost—
"Ah, bejays, ain't she sweeter than lavender salts?"

"Lord's bones, is it Easter?" cries Mabel O'Lannihan.
"Come follow the leader!" Obedient dames
Spill out of their beds and in shaky formation
On slippered feet shiver their fragile old frames

As they dance in a conga line on down the corridor
After Mabel the leader, who casts a sly look
Round the corner—on, on past the nurses' station
Where the night nurse nods on her open logbook,

On, on to the ward where the menfolk are sleeping
Like cordwood stacked. Mabel waves a game leg,
Crying "Up! Come a-dancing! 'Tis Easter morning!
Last man on the dance floor's a chickenless egg!"

Now Timothy Mudge, who's perpetually shaking,
Not known to have noticed a thing in years,

Takes such a to-do that he coughs his teeth out,
Cups liver-splotched hands to his overgrown ears.

A hoot and a chuckle from Joshua Finver,
That sour old cynic who got in Dutch
For giving the dime-pinching dietician
Such a bash on the backside he shattered his crutch—

"So what are you dancing for, Mabel O'Lannihan?
The nature of things goes from awful to worse.
What's the moon but a piss in a porcelain basin?
Hear the years grind their gears like a secondhand hearse!

"So why should I cling like a leech to living
In fear of a fall that will fracture a hip,
Trapped, strapped in a wheelchair, kept under sedation?
To be told by a nurse's aide, 'None of your lip?'"

Says Mabel, "Why sit on your lazy ass bitching
In your moth-eaten bathrobe and you catching chills?
You've plenty of room for a big second helping.
Come dance with me now, you old bottle of pills.

"Ah, the last child I had is long buried before me—
Get a load of this leg, it still knows how to traipse.
What have I to fear from the here and hereafter?
I'm no virgin in Hell, to be leading apes."

She whooshes dust clouds from a still turntable
That at last is to be for the first time played,
Tosses on a Strauss waltz, cries. "Listen to Mabel!
Up, up on your pins! Were you born afraid?"

Now out on the floor move the hesitant dancers:
And two-fingered Fein bows to Mag O'Quinn.
Tim Mudge finds his feet, takes a break from quaking,
Screws his courage to sticking point, soon cuts in.

Now women and men into dance steps stumble,
All hatched from the shells of their separate woes.
Their crutches and walkers and canes forgotten,
With slow steps they weave the design of a rose.

"Circle round!" hollers Mabel. "Once more now, me dearies!
You wheezing old engines, set wheels to the track!"
In the thud of their heavy steps nobody notices
Finver slump to the floor with a last heart attack.

Now the noise of their party has wakened the night nurse.
In she comes at a gallop. Her blood congeals,
And beholding the rumpus she drops her thermometer—
The mercury dashes for cover. She squeals,

"What are you dancing for, Mabel O'Lannihan,
With your chilblains and bedsores, your breakable legs?

You take one more step and I'm calling the doctor!
Stop, stop, or I'll dock you your chocolate eggs!"

"I'm dancing," says Mabel, "to keep me from dying.
It's no sort of a Sunday to stay in a tomb.
This world is the worse for a shortage of dancing.
Stand back, you old pill, give me plenty of room!"

They thunder the floorboards and shiver the rafters.
While the night nurse ogles in shock and surprise
The horde of them move, celebrating this morning
Of the risen Christ's rooster-red Easter eyes.

Jews

I meet a Jew, we always hit it off,
Outsiders that we are. We tend to band
Together separately. We understand
Each not belonging to the other's club,

Excluding me from Talmud, Yom Kippur,
Uncircumcised as I'm, born far from folks
Who struggled in a ghetto. Different strokes,
That's us. But meat a rabbi's blade makes pure,

Chopped chicken liver, challah, macaroons
Nest in my hungry mouth like home sweet home.
I feel a long way now from Peter's Rome
And somehow nearer to Jerusalem,

To Jewish laughter: when a baby's bladed,
His first ten percent cut. "Is that the highest
In the church a boy can go? Just Pope? Not
Christ? So why not? One of *our* boys made it."

Surrounded by a neighborhood that pays
Jesus lip-service—maybe it annoys

Them just a bit? They don't complain. We goys
Infect their children with our special days:

Some Jewish tots believe in Santa Claus
And coax for stockings, gifts on Christmas eve,
With chocolate Easter bunnies stuff their jaws—
Legends that fewer Christians still believe.

And yet the Jews I know don't seem to mind.
They have one up on me. More centuries past
Remain their heritage. My lucky kind
Haven't been herded, shipped to death camps, gassed.

Easter Parade in Sorrento

At last it nears,
Blurting a funeral march
On clarinet and trombone, whamming drums,
Piercing the crowd-clogged street,
The Black Procession of Good Friday night:

Four hundred torch-lit figures sable-robed,
Hooded, bearing the pall
Of the slain Christ. Here comes the Virgin caped
In mourning. Now advance
Some with reflecting silver trays to hold
Huge crucifixion implements: two dice,
A stuffed cock that for Peter might have crowed,
Severed centurion ears awaiting Christ's
Order to reattach, red-headed lance
That pierced His side, rope loop to goad
Judas to suicide.

Not all the pious have obeyed the Pope
Since long ago he threatened to withhold
The sacraments from all
Supporters of the Risorgimento.

Rules and decrees, not ingrained centuries-old

Feelings, dissolve and fade,

For eyes still glisten as this grim parade

Circles a worn brick plaza *lento, lento.*

6 Last Acts

Departure

With thoughtful steps, made certain that no friend
Would catch the drift of what she planned to do:
Bringing each correspondence to an end
Not giving the least hint that it was through.
Paying the last bill from the paper boy
And stopping his deliveries. She would break
No trust. She'd always tried not to annoy
People, even herself. Her one mistake
Was looking in the mirror as she died
And though the gunshot had been carefully placed
It struck her that to lie there found by men,
The careful powder of her face defaced,
Would violate at last her long-kept pride,
But there was no more she could do just then.

In the Motel Office

Where do you think you're going?

Just out back—

I thought I'd give a tap on Number Four

And see if he's still ticking.

Jesus, Jack,

What's this, a hospital we're running here?

I bet there's dough or something in his bags.

Used underwear, you mean.

And something better. Christ,

You see him sign in? Face all gray? He drags

Like one whole side of him is paralyzed

And coughs up black blood on the frigging pen

And when he breaks his wallet out the green

Is like he robbed a bank.

Dreaming again! Another get-rich-quick. I never seen
A guy like you.

You mean a guy that claims

The chips left lying around. Be nice and Pappy

Might take you out to Vegas for some games

If this poor jerk is dead.

Well make it snappy.

Pudge Wescott

Pudge Wescott, you were what they call short-changed,
But when you tended your stepfather's store
Your stories didn't strike me as deranged—
How once your pal the pimp tossed you a whore;
That summer job you signed up for by phone
Not knowing it was nudists till you looked:
A lovely girl with nothing on walked by
Your downcast eyes while you short-order cooked.

Your old man couldn't stand you. So he scored
Some papers, packed you off to Greystone Park,
Declared a mental case, the county's ward.
I wonder were you frightened of the dark
And did you know fellow patients? Ginsberg's mad
Mother Naomi, Woody Guthrie willing
To strum tunes with a visitor, a lad
Who called himself Bob Dylan?

I saw the news and felt a body blow.
You'd smashed a window making your escape.
They found you lying face down in the snow,
Eyes staring straight at nothing, mouth agape.

So here's to you, Pudge Wescott, for you meant
Well all your days, which soon enough were gone.
You never quite knew what was going on
And gave up puzzling over it, and went.

Tourist Taking Pictures of Children in Mali

In a dust-cluttered back street of Bamako
The tourist halts, collects a yelping pack
By granting them an instant picture show:
Behold! their faces in his camera's back!

Whooping, they crowd in, overjoyed to spot
A crony framed in liquid crystal display,
A naked little sister. It's their lot
To live unphotographed until this day

When a vacationing wizard from the sky
Brings them a glowing screen in which to peer,
An instrument beyond their means to buy,
Whose cost might feed a family for a year.

A chill besets the tourist. Now he feels
His hands upon his Pentax clamp like locks
Lest it be stolen; now he blithely steals
These children, captives in his light-tight box.

Rush Hour

Bumper to bumper, homebound cars
File down the street at daylight's fail,
A line of circus elephants,
Each trunk clasped to the next one's tail.

Now flaring red imperatives
Of stoplights interrupt their creep,
But soon the column gives a lurch
Like giants waking up from sleep.

The rigors of commuter law
Decree that they move homeward slowly
To what awaits? A bale of straw
Or love and frozen ravioli?

Rummage Sale

Here are the dregs of bookshelves cast aside:
Book of the Month Club choices now refused,
The memoirs of some general swelled with pride,
Labor-intensive cookbooks still unused—

The castoffs of a season of demeaning,
Cleared from the house relentlessly as sweepers
Rout dust clouds in a merciless spring cleaning.
Book buyers these folks were, but not book keepers.

I wonder at this thick tome's long regress,
Hacked out by one whose fame and sales were stellar,
Now cast down from the tower of success
To molder in a spiderwebbed best cellar.

How It Happens

for Seth Wheeler

Yes, poems can write themselves—that happens when
The poet feels picked up, used like a pen.
In my whole life that's happened—when? ten times?
Far oftener, a poem suggests its rhymes,
Grants me a word with which a word might mate,
A seed to plant and carefully cultivate.
Hard work runs head-first up against resistance,
For who can will a poem into existence?
You have to wait with patience and believe,
Camp by your keyboard, ready to receive,
Letting no option prematurely shut.
The moral may well be *Sit on your butt.*

At Eighty

We go on drawing close as we resist
The sneak attacks of wily wear and tear,
Feeling each day reducing us to grist
For doctors' mills, mere grain for Medicare.

Comrades in dissolution, we behold
The hesitant sunlight ray by ray advance
And lashes of hard rain and sharp-toothed cold
Wreak havoc on our newly planted plants.

But isn't there a sweetness in this sense
That moments count for more, now that we strive
To drag our heels downhill while mending rents,
Finding content in waking still alive?
Lord, may our progress fall prey to correction
As we keep heading down by indirection.

NOTES

Lonesome George. In the summer of 2011, my wife Dorothy and I met this famous resident of the Galápagos Islands, a giant land turtle kept in a pen at the Darwin Research Center. He was said to be the last member of his subspecies. Despite many attempts to persuade him to mate, George had shown no interest in reproducing. Perhaps his indifference might have been due to his age: he was believed to be at least a hundred years old.

For a moment as I stared at him, I had the sense that he was looking back at me. I may have imagined this, but I felt that between us two old codgers nearing the end, there was a certain sympathy. In June 2012, a few days after this poem appeared in a magazine, George died, leaving no progeny.

Three Saints: Martha. The Tarasque, a dragonlike monster of legend, lion-headed and part fish, was said to have terrorized the people of Tarascon in Provence until Martha subdued it by confronting it with a crucifix and sprinkling it with holy water.

Thomas Hardy's Obsequies. This story was told by a guide showing tour parties through Hardy's house, Max Gate, in Dorsetshire. He strongly affirmed the truth of it.

Last Poem (after Robert Desnos). A member of the French Resistance, Desnos was arrested by the Gestapo in February 1944. A Polish student found him dying of typhus among survivors of Buchenwald, discovered this final poem, and sent it to the poet's wife.

ACKNOWLEDGMENTS

Thanks are due to the editors and poetry editors of these
publications where poems first appeared, some in earlier
versions.

American Journal of Poetry (Robert Nazarene): "Jews"
The Atlantic (David Barber): "Lonesome George"
Calamaro (Anthony Harrington): "Early Morning in Turks and
    Caicos Hospital"
Chautauqua (Richard Foerster): "Thomas Hardy's Obsequies"
Chronicles (Catharine Savage Brosman): "At Eighty," "Literacy"
Columbia Magazine (Eric McHenry): "Tourist Taking Pictures of
    Children in Mali"
French Leave: Translations (Robert L. Barth, publisher): "Abyss"
    (after Charles Baudelaire), "Pierrot's Soliloquy" (after Jules
    Laforgue), "Sonnet for Hélène" (after Pierre de Ronsard)
The Hopkins Review (John T. Irwin): "Disabled Music," "Jane
    Austen Drives to Alton in Her Donkey Trap," "My Bohemia: A
    Fantasy" (after Arthur Rimbaud), "The Odors of New Jersey"
The Hudson Review (Paula Deitz): "Catherine," "Hopes"
Ibbetson Street (Harris Gardner): "Nicholas," "Pudge Wescott,"
    "Rush Hour"
Measure (Rob Griffith and Paul Bone): "Departure"
Modern European Poetry, published by Bantam Books (Patricia
    Terry, editor of French translations): "Last Poem" (after
    Robert Desnos), "Mortal Landscape" (after Robert Sabatier)
Negative Capability (Sue Brannan Walker): "Invitation to the
    Dance," "Rummage Sale"
The New Statesman (Anthony Thwaite): "Sea Breeze" (after
    Stéphane Mallarmé)
Poetry (John Frederick Nims): "A Word from Hart Crane's Ghost"
Raintown Review (Anna M. Evans): "Martha"

Rosebud (John E. Smelcer): "My Mother Consigns to the Flames
My Trove of Comic Books"
Third Wednesday (Lawrence W. Thomas): "Riposte"
Trinacria (Joseph S. Salemi): "Because the Dinner Meat Was
Done to Death" (after Stéphane Mallarmé)

About the Author

X. J. KENNEDY adopted his pen name to be different from better known Joe Kennedys. Before becoming a full-time writer, he taught at the University of Michigan, the University of North Carolina–Greensboro, Tufts University, Wellesley College, the University of California–Irvine, and Leeds University. He has written nine collections of verse, among them *In a Prominent Bar in Secaucus: New & Selected Poems, 1955–2007*, a notable book of the American Library Association, and *Fits of Concision: Collected Poems of Six or Fewer Lines*. He is the author of twenty-three books for children. The National Association of Teachers of English has given him their award for children's poetry; the American Academy and Institute of Arts and Letters, their prize for light verse. *An Introduction to Poetry*, now in a thirteenth edition and coauthored with Dana Gioia, has been used by more than four million students. A comic novel, *A Hoarse Half-human Cheer*, has been widely ignored. He and wife Dorothy live in Lexington, Massachusetts.

For his verse Kennedy has received the Poets' Prize, the Robert Frost Medal of the Poetry Society of America, the Aiken-Taylor Award from the University of the South, and in 2015 the Jackson Poetry Prize from Poets & Writers. The judges of the latter award, Heather McHugh, Vijay Seshadri, and Deborah Warren, commended Kennedy for "translating the human predicament into poetry perfectly balancing wit, savagery, and compassion. The size of his poems may be small, but their scope is vast."

Poetry Titles in the Series